Pra

"I am overwhelmed ~, _ _ ,
expressed in this collection, but even more so by her
profound recognition of Ancestor worship and their
essential connection to our existence in the now and in
the future. These poems, as she acknowledges, are not of
her voice but of the ancestors speaking of our duty to
them that we cannot escape. ... A continuation of her
eternal moan and praise to ancestors, asking, pleading,
praying. She is the new truth of the old truth. She is
tribal history and eternity."
    -Marvin X
    author of *How to Recover from the Addiction to
    White Supremacy*, and *The Wisdom of Plato Negro:
    A Hustler's Guide to the Game Called Life*

"Ayodele is a profoundly gifted artist whose creations
take on many forms - from community building to
directing to writing and educating (and much more!).
She has gravitas and grace and has amassed quite a local
following. It is her command of words, and poetry
mixed with her unique perspective that makes her work
stirring, beautiful and poignant."
    -Amanda Bornstein
    co-founder of The Flight Deck Art Gallery and
    Theater

"This is the essence of poetry: a recalcitrant and
unapologetic collection of verse. The words and meter
flow through the pages. To hear the artist herself or to
indulge one's imagination alone, the work identifies
beauty and injustice and tries to create a place for itself
amidst the successes and failures of our sorely imperfect
humanity."
    -Zack Dye
    author of *21st Century Coastal American Verses*

Incandescent

Ayodele Nzinga

Also by Ayodele Nzinga

Books

Performing Literacy:
A Narrative Inquiry into Performance Pedagogy in a
Marginalized Community

Singles

"Don't Call Me" – J. Definitely
"Bigger Picture" – Inspire
"Hood Affair" – Playa Righteous
"Look n the Glass" – Playa Righteous
"WordznBulletz" – We Inhale
"Freedom" – Hairdoo
"Pocket Full of Cowries" – Wolf Hawk Jaguar
"Prosperity Movement" – Wolf Hawk Jaguar
"Water" — Oshunfemi Njeri

Compilations

"Lower Bottom Playaz Hood Mix" – Compilation-We
Inhale

Albums

The SorrowLand Rebellion – Black Apes Music

Incandescent

Copyright © 2021 by Ayodele Nzinga

All rights reserved.

Published in the United States by
Not a Pipe Publishing
www.NotAPipePublishing.com

Trade Paperback Edition

ISBN-13: 978-1-948120-89-0

Contents

Forward by K.M. Smith

I love words. The taste of them, the feel and especially the sight of them. I wrap myself in lyrical, multisyllabic words, reveling in the music and the lilt of words that dance like *conjurer* and undulate like *transmutation* or vibrate like *praisesong*. I am both dazed and delighted by the snap of *fly* and the flash of *pain* or the simple ease of *joy*. Staccato rhythms. Languid flourishes. The very gift of breathing is celebrated when we have access to words. Words that are crafted and nurtured, that are curated and caressed, that pulse with life and death and everything in between. We are blessed and cursed and then consecrated because poets are gods who hold the power of persuasion and brilliance and illumination. When they're good.

Incandescent, the brilliance of expression that Ayodele Nzinga has so lovingly crafted, is red hot in its urgency. It moves subtly, it shifts and crescendos and somersaults across time and space, through light and darkness, joy and pain. This fiery book of poetry comes at you quickly. Questions abound and answers permeate about justice and freedom and existence.

something
is
always
dying
minutes murder hours every
sunrise light cuts dark

rage & bullets next to
the hope in the drawer

And just as you begin to catch your breath, as you ponder your own collusion in and ignorance of injustices small and large, she pivots to soothe your senses, caress your breaking heart, bolster your connection to this life, to love, to your ancestors.

under the blue moon
we shift shapes
baptize at transformations
rematerialize over gravesites
translate
game
etched in concrete
dreaming
wholeness as a possibility

Incandescent will shake you by the shoulders then embrace you in revolutionary love; abiding and vibrational, Nzinga propels us forward into light, into incandescence. The passion for our people is palpable and alluring, sometimes maternal and sometimes seductive. The fierce way
that she loves and heals and educates and upholds and builds and wallows is revolutionary. And explosive. And complex. And liberatory in every sense.

This *Incandescent* is a love offering. Nzinga's heart has exploded on these pages, inviting you to act and to see and to feel. These poems reckon with family and joy, speak of struggle and insurgency, extol ecstasy.

say you got red hot lovin daddy
well
rock yo mama til
the meat fall
off the bone

As you sit with these poems, reading and rereading, learning and growing, laughing and crying, notice the exaltation. Lean into the pleasurable places that are tough and soft. Allow these words to dance about in your own heart and mind. Believe, again, in liberation. And healing. And possibility. And your sister.

Incandescent is like fire: it is controlled heat and scorches so that it can clear the way for new growth. Be cautious. Be curious. Be transported.

in the solitude of her ascension
she awaits the second
chorus of the fire song
the notes
building in the wind
soon another climb begins

K.M. Smith
Oakland, CA.
January, 2021

Introduction by Marvin X

I am pleased to write this introduction to Ayodele's latest collection. I am overwhelmed by the pervasive African love expressed in this collection, but even more so by her profound recognition of Ancestor worship and their essential connection to our existence in the now and in the future. These poems, as she acknowledges, are not of her voice but of the ancestors speaking of our duty to them that we cannot escape. She begins with "The Accounting" that is a challenge to us all, what will you do, what will you be? Do you think you cannot be? No, cannot be, you must be, you have no choice as ancestor Amiri Baraka said to me, "Do I have a choice?" I always answered him, "No!"

In truth, even the soldiers of Prophet Muhammad (PBUH) threw down their weapons and ran in the heat of battle. In our times even the Black Panther Party soldiers in battle with the Oakland pigs when they murdered Lil' Bobby Hutton, threw down their guns and ran. Oh, yes, you can run but you can't hide, no hiding place the Bible tells us.

"One Love" speaks of divine unity, yes, we are in God and God is in us as the Sufi teach, especially Guru Bawa, Holy Master. But this poem is her approach to Divine Love and human love that is inescapable for those who know.

"Mama Connie's Poem" is a continuation of ancestor praise, the dominant theme of this collection. Her lines remind me of my lines as per ancestors, "Don't you hear them calling, saying rise up, be free, don't give up, rise up, be free?"

"Awake": A dream poem from her granddaughter in the night, channeling again the ancestors to do right. Again, Ayodele is steeped in ancestor spirits.

"Word Affair": A poetic linguistic deconstruction of language or words, words that heal, kill, joyful words, love words, sound words, screams, hollar words, word colors, spitting words, contradictions, word music, and finally, words only a poet can understand or a lover of poetry.

"Wade in the Water": A continuation of her eternal moan and praise to ancestors, asking, pleading, praying. She is the new truth of the old truth. She is tribal history and eternity.

--Marvin X
3/12/21

the accounting

when wolves & sheep
are counted
when scales are finally balanced
when justice can see
when the clarion sounds
& good men come forth
where
will you be
when the times of
camels & needles eyes
is upon us like a coat in
winter will you be with us
or constricted by the sins of your fathers
your own sins
the smell of insatiable greed
eyes closed
deaf to the sound of
children
forest oceans dying
when it all falls down
& it will
where
will you be
when the false cover of innocence
is obliterated & we are naked
with
what we did & did not do
what we let transpire in our name

what we pushed against profited from let occur
did not stop
lived with considered collateral
when the price is extracted for standing
by when both innocence & ignorance are
not recognized as a defense for
bloodied hands
where
will you be
when you understand some stains
can't be removed
where are you
now
while the air trembles
with purpose
choose
life or death
choose
we are interconnected bound
by blood
twisted like coils of dna
we are one as surely
as there is only one sky
what happens to one will
fall like plague upon all
dig one hole
dig two
the second for you
where
will you be
when right prevails
& it will
where

will you be
when the cups are righted
the books are done
& the cost demanded
for what you wrought
with the breath in your lungs
when the prayer enacted by
your hands has
a life of its own
where

will you be

no apologies

i offer no apology
for my tone
the tilt of my head
my gaze
embracing of my intellect
or my clear thought
not one
god gave 'em to me
deal wit 'em

one love

love
perfected
is generous
one
is divine
undivided whole
one perfect love
love purely perfect
from soul
to souls
traveling the same road
together in the storm
the same with splendid
difference the same
heart
same struggle
fear
same pain
joy
same dreams
night mares
together on the road
walking the same way
hands in the air
mouths open singing life
out of the lean spaces we stand in
out of the thin air we breathe
out of the courage we possess
we are all we have

standing on the bones
remembering when the sky
was cleared & the thunder
was our friend the earth our provider
the sun our light us multiplying
one perfect love
unfolding
like a rose or
a diaspora traded for a mother's arms
we are everywhere together in
the no where wanting for our
brothers what we want for ourselves
one love
one perfect love
bigger than the oceans that separate us
as vast as the story that connects us
deeper than melanin
inbred racial memory
binding as blood
love perfected
we are one
indivisible from the inside
one love
one
one perfect love

mama connie's poem

scent in a room
can
pull me back
through time
sometimes
it's a song truth is i can
be interrupted in the middle of
a thought the ancestors
call clearer than a phone line
ringing they want to talk through me
they want to say something
they need a tongue i give them mine
today they want you to know there is
nothing new there have always been stars
we are cosmic dust fragments of all
that has ever been there is nothing new
only those who have forgotten
those who think this is all
now is not all here is not all they want
us to know there is nothing new
nothing unthought only unknown in the now
they want us to remember to remember
they say it's important
there are things that get lost
the sound of someone's laughter a gift
from on high forgotten floating somewhere
wanting to be remembered the sweat of a brow
furrowed in concentration falling into the dirt

to become a part of the all carried in the wind to
rain down again absorbed forever waiting for
its moment to be recalled the curve of a muscle
strained in burden holding lifting making the now
i stand in honoring that toil that honest labor often
free unrewarded but earnest there are stories of quiet
saturday mornings in the back seats of cars
no money but going somewhere looking seeing longing
for some future time not knowing those
precious moments would disappear under the weight
of those future days long & empty of the things
that rolled softly before them or were drug down long
dark
hallways some lost on purpose others waiting
for thought to brush up against them
things like
the sound of your dead great grandmother's name
gasping for air
waiting for you
to say it aloud
they want us to know we are their future
yes the dead have futures
we live them
they want us to know they left work for us
they want us to remember
what they tried but could not do
all that was dreamed
they want us to do it they want us to know we
are a promise they dream on
yes the dead have dreams
we are their dreams our rising our falling
our pain our joy

they want us to know
they told me to
write it down & say it aloud
i am writing it down
i will say it aloud

awake

the phone is ringing
in the middle of the night
she is miles away
my beautiful granddaughter
a piece of moonlight
shining in another part of the world
she is all tears frustration pours through
the phone line she has called to share
the fact that she is awake no longer asleep
her eyes are open her dreams have changed
she woke up with freedom on her mind
she has discovered herself
she got the call
the one we know can come at anytime
reminding us of the story

word affair

know the weight of a word
its secret depths
ninja stars
better to hurl some
some are to be cried
marking space & time
non retractable
forever
others moaned
some whispered
some only uttered
quietly
mindful of the
would be sayer
cuz
nomo is powerful mojo
hoodoo on high
don't work for
just anybody
got borders
need papers
translations are
all approximate
Inner-standings
break contracts
form new agreements
loose cement
with internal compasses
yeah

see son scat words
inflict wounds only jazz
rifts heal false love words
drowned in tears words
living on their own
strolling naked
waiting for you
at sunrise
textured colored unsaid
pregnant with purpose
Intended in integrity
used well
swallowed whole
spit venomously dripping healing
slipping carelessly
fraught with innuendo
leaning casually in its
own shade
undoing you
formally
rented
written by another
now haunting you
arranging the space
deleting endings
beginning again
speaking over you
changing the story
spilling like
sunlight
sneaky building blocks
raining jumping

skipping with razors
cross pages
writing our lives

wade in the water

across a large body of water
i came from home
across a large body of water
filled with my ancestors bones
ancestors whisper
stack the bones
one atop the other
walk across the water
home
/?/can i go
home
changed
i left
i can never go home again
If i found me
i could not speak to myself
i do not remember the tribe
or
the village
my blood mixed many times
i am a new tribe
israelite
13th tribe of judah
lost tribe of shabazz
north 'merican african
in the land
i helped build
still exotic
alien
i can never go home again

there is no picture of me on the altar
remembered
only by ghosts
who haunt holding pens
longed for more by the bones
than others from home
i stopped claiming you
said
louisiana, alabama, mississippi
when asked
about home
when they ask me
about home
i look at the water & cry
watching the waves
their rocking movement
whisper from the
remembrance of ships
slipping through known
reality
depositing
my soul on the other side
i can never go home again
home
is the ocean floor
with the carver & the priest
the bones of the spear maker
& the last cry of
the greatest hunter of leopard
that ever lived
home is in the blood

woven in the kinte
in the mud
lost
a primal scream before death
burn of salt
water in lungs
lost forever severed
home gone
long time now
i can't go back home
we should have dug our feet
in the mud and fought
we should have burnt the ships
stole the whips
? why didn't you come for me
i would have stayed where i had a *family* name
? if i stack the ancestors dreams
i can build a bridge
can my soul come home
can i walk on soil
forefathers owned
sit my burdens down &
be welcomed home

manless blue

they cry
the mothers
alone
with children
tears
over flat beer
cheap meat
crying on therapist couches
on the sofas of mediums
in the supermall
the spa
they cry hoarse
urgent rivers
sprung from
leaky chasms in souls
crying for men
who have left
men come too late
who would not
could not be
were not true
men
that lied
left them without
love joy hope
maybes
carefully wrapped should haves
no more half
just alone

with out
outside
without
protectors fathers
lovers husbands
no men
where are our men
they cry
the sisters
without brothers
cry
as no one comes to the rescue
pulls them on to shoulders
to view a world of could be
can come true
if you got the nerve to dream it
no one to say
that's not a weed
that's my sister
she just ain't flowered yet
where are the men children
brotherpeople
the men
who
think you are special
know your worst secrets
& don't care
the brothers the sisters need
the brothers
brothers cry for
to show them
the potential perfect

love they seek
where are the brothermen mentor guides
where are the sons
tall & proud
singing the name of
fathers
honoring the love of
mothers
being brothers
to daughters
of proud parents
the sons
who increase
the tribe
the blessings of this house
where are the men they cry
children without fathers
lost without yang caught
off balance without nets
free falling
in the hands of
manless women
whose tears they can not wade on
whose prayers fall short
whose pain is unending
as again
& again
they lose men
/?/where are the me
we cry
in the face of sliding downhill

deaf dumb and guilty
of nothing
no sin
greater than inaction
we collectively
pause
waiting for
the men
while
we suffer the man
waiting for the men
where are our men
the standing few cry
thin in number
their cries echoing
where is my brother
where is my father
where is my son
where
are the men
are they on the
mountain plotting our salvation
down by the water planning any means necessary
are they marching on the shore eyes
on the north star
hearts souls minds
on zion
/?/where are the men

this woman

woman
female as spanish guitar
curved intricately
complex notes resounding from
a soul composed of
music
woman
soft as diamonds
no pale anemic untried virgin
full bloom fragrant intoxicating
female of an ancient
order of sublime souls
raw creation
groaning life into existence
I arch my back throw back
my head
the universe contracts
pregnant
with my expectations
my open hand tickles the belly of the
horizon
as i inhale my dreams risen
from the altars of my effort
some dashing
crystalline /forlorn
on the shores of my
regrets
i am
kin to the beginning

of beginnings
begetting infinity
life nile
pulsing in the veins of
the galaxy
enigma shrouded in
the elemental simplicity of
sunrise
in the middle of the night

altered

we bow
stop to deify
we carry
pieces of bone
hanks of hair
rocks from a place
they walked
wood from the
tree
the box was
carved from
images framed
in silver
our life
before this time
we honored our
lives
with talisman
of life
to guide
in the
new dark
we brought
our
ancestors
to live in our houses
seeking their
ase to shine

on us
in us
through us
turned out of the
gourd blowing
in wind turned
perpetual storm
pressed into
forgetting
not remembering
confusing
letting go
spilling on strange ground
concrete holding us
as corners cradle us
altars spring forth
pop ups
temporal here in the
no where lost
constellations of
rancid weeds
too soon
souls
force flown
to
deity returned
freed by fire
that heals or kills
rude cosmic returns
not soft
memory
jagged honorings

blood
sanctified
with
courvoisier remy
epithets tagged
on
fences fail to divide
us from
memories of oceans
falling falling falling
no
where
to land
trading crowns
for
t shirt legends
silkscreened prayers
r i p at souls
abandoned among the living
like a language
spoken once
dimly remembered
struggling not
to be forgotten
gross bouquets
tragically merry
color on grey
ravaged streets
disturb the corners
of troubled minds
define the contours of broken hearts

ancestors pray for us
open a road in
the dark for us
blackeyed
peas collard
greens
great grandma's hands
on us

approaching zion

she shook the dust from her feet
arched her back
stretched her soul towards the heavens
her palms open
her long fingers extended

she shook stars from her hair
dancing a redemption dance
on the mountaintop

it had been a long climb
there were larger mountains in the distance
begging her foot falls
looked on with only
the slightest yearning in her eyes
her heart holding this place
etched on her soul
the valley
below

there were those in the valley
& on the mountains
in the distance
that feared her leaving
dread her coming
her footsteps will echo soon
on paths not often tread
by those from the valley
she inhales savoring the evenness

of this plateau

in the solitude of her ascension
she awaits the second
chorus of the fire song
the notes
building in the wind
soon another climb begins

she is weary but inspired
by the possibilities unfolding
she hears the music
growing in the breeze

she continues to ascend,
her face towards zion

ashes of dream

...it didn't matter that the dreams had been smoked
only that the bag was empty
and no conjurer was at hand
to pray an absolution
tomorrow was yet to be danced uphill

there were holes in the strategy
of waiting patiently
walking out in the road
looking at the horizon was better
one must court new dreams
if they are to come to you
let alone come
true

...it didn't matter that the dreams had been wasted
only that there were no more
to pose with in the window
contemplating the texture of intentions
served crisp with pale white pear wine
then
ignored

there is no anointing on the wind for the dreamless

baby's horn

(for adijuhan)

when baby plays that horn
birds sit down to listen
tall girls dance slowly
grown men cry
when baby plays his horn
small boys whistle
youngsters snap their fingers
old ladies close their eyes sigh
when baby plays his horn
his brow glistens
his hands caress
his eyes cloud over
when baby plays his horn
i open
wider than the fattest notes
& smile
when baby plays his horn

berkeley flea at ashby bart

hot afternoon in late august
or sometimes in early october
in berkeley
the trees are few
the heat radiates up
off the asphalt in ripples
like long grass on an africkan
savannah far away in my memory
the drummers drum
some ancient melody
scribed in their blood
by ancient rhythm older than
the city they drum in
some in the raiment of their ancestors
others dress in the robes of their new tribes
we come to see & be seen
we come to buy & to sell
come to haggle & present the
old alongside the new
the worthless & the priceless
side by side like some ancient market
in some other time
sometimes dancers dance
or poets recite & we are in
congo square far away
laying down burdens
rearranging rhythms
reaching for something
living just under our surfaces

we circle
seeing what we have seen before
paying attention or ignoring
as our needs dictate
we eat platters of fruit
sample scented oil
pay too little
pay too much
barter & trade
recreate worth
continue tradition
create our own legend
on long sunday afternoons
in earliest october
or sometimes late august
at the berkeley flea

blue moon

we sit in surreal
blue moonlight
serenely solid
squared off
shot callers
survivors of battles
stripes & stars
o. g.s' burning trees
sipping yak
in a square circle
under the willow
only fire missing
to mark the scared
nature of this
ancient circle
youth
good & bad
speak
respectful tones
punctuating verbal jousts
between vets

the good linger
the bad break wide
game chopped
order painted on chaos
making sense of the world
one hood at a time

warriors tales & admonitions conveying
collective ancestral wisdom
shooting light & laces for the system
we wake em up or give em up for twisted
this vantage
grieves casualties never listed
we here
exceptions to the usual case
retired slaves escaped
but some are sewn to the dark
ain't no light
in some houses
the o.g.'s square circle
no flames but lit
extended family fire
warms even
the coldest desperados
under the blue moon
we shift shapes
baptize
the transmuted
fruits of
transformations
mapmakers
holders of the keys
translators of game
etched in concrete
hood royalty
freely dreaming
wholeness as a possibility

blues joint

roll me like a joint.
rock me,
like i got no bones.
say you got red hot lovin
honey man
bring it on
say
you got red-hot lovin daddy
well
rock yo mama till
the meat fall
off the bone.
show me why
i won't let you leave me alone
roll me like a joint.
rock me,
like i got no bones

transmutation

living with the weight
was a blessing as some
crushed easily or never
sought to stand up to
where life live easy waiting
bent crooked forever
dipping lower
getting trapped in a story
with a tragic end
for someone
dreams become
can't even recognize
that boy no more
that kinda carry not
the same as living
bowed down
like that
no sky
getting by
survive weighs
more
than other words
with more room
inside torment
is a poor guide
have you slipping
in the darkness you
conjure trying to
get over / overcome
still
be breathing in the

morning getting trough
the 13th straight
night with no stars
everyday
ever anywhere your
bent soul aims itself
banging on
karma all guns blazing
she keep slapping you
& the small voice
whispering
that challenges you
casually suggesting
upright is always
a possibility even
on a deathbed
but it do
play better with a
track record we know
by patterns like birds
migrating we know
from repetition
for its own sake
sometimes it cuts
pray unused luck
from your grandfather
can find its way
through half promises &
demands more from you
it's there
if we check for it
better can be a habit

the voice in your ear
the rider on the shoulder
who knows you know
reminds you to stand
up straight even if
you snap trying get
the bend out ya back
get right is serious
wants dedication
make you walk
like you going somewhere
remembers where its
been trying to get you here
where you are tall
dues paid to overpaid
willingly righted
puzzle piece
finding the place
absolution made
right can fill
cracked vessels
leaking encouraging
lessons worn like
robes or scars that
remind you to remember
transmutation
alchemy ritual rebirth
own the
bending before rising
the path was
always
waiting

cracked code

compound complex fractures
to the psyche one hundred miles
an hour fireflies on the dashboard
blueberries & cherries in the rearview
& i am still behind
those warm wrapped in cotton
comfort softly sleeping dreaming
soy lattes no keys
for the car
don't matter
there is no engine
a present from the government
to insure i arrive on time
for my failure to rise
confusion woke me
dreaming someone else's dream
of an ill fitting suit i could
not shrink into
they followed the trail of
stars falling from my hair
i became a long
distance runner cloaked in
a north star frame of mind
didn't matter they ate
the moss off the trees
the path remembered me
hounded by blueberries & cherries
rabid dogs in the swamp

defenders of property & crooked
lives lawless law screaming
lay down dead don't make
me shoot you stop resisting
being invisible they
will never see me coming
in my dreams
when i fall i learn to fly
in my grandparents
dreams i was
born flying
it's the song
from the graveyard
in the ocean
that wakes
me in the midst
of falling stars
i claim myself
remembering to remember
planted like
a tree
only sky above
my godz favor
me & thunder some
like gin others
rum the drum
vibrates the wind
the path is cleared
before my ile
the child guards the road
red shango
over the front door

i walk in ire
nah you don't want
trouble we

out the closet
whyte
smelling of cotton eyez
lit by torchlight
the redeemer
come to lift the dream
what never was
exceptional
manifest
natural selection
pushing the purchase
of fire power
bang bang
hurly burly
the bear is here
end result of wolves
in cadillacs with lambo upgrades
crazy in the daylight
rubbing your eyes
will not change the channel
normal insanity
interrupted for naked
mayhem

look see

she say
you got to see
further than looking

it got lost in the
crowd everybody turnt
backwards/eyes closed
trying to understand
how today got here

ain't no pennies in the drawer
the dresser lives on the sidewalk

the sidewalk is melting
don't look maybe you won't fall through
you remember
ain't nothing underneath
even the graveyard moved
you forgot everything
too late now

pennies pay the ferryman
hope lives on the other side
of the river think hard
it might stick out
charts lucky powder & time
how did today get here

the face in the mirror got starz

for eyez

wolves in lamborghinis
issue orders for new
worlds crane & bulldozer dream
neocolonial blueprints for
a cultural renaissance
bones ground into feathers
trending
on ebay & etsy

all artists report immediately
to homeland security
rfp's required before
completing your current thought

? where are your blueprints

they didn't see the crash
coming chasing the wave
overhead underwater after
pawning the guns & rage
your breath on the outside
of the window
steaming the surface
you wrote your name
the sun came up on
your dresser living on the sidewalk
you broke the mirror
because your grandfather kept
trying to escape with those
northstar eyez

praise song turned
'merican bluz fingers
move looking for pennies
in the drawer speaking hope
like fragments of language forgotten
in shards of mirror
on melted sidewalk
roots in a pouch hanging
near your rib cage
dangling from
the cord suspended
from your third eye

unfinished prayers

i died
one thousand times
in the valley
trying to feed my life

i keep drowning in a
world on fire only
poems form the
ocean to ground me

i want to be a tree
eyes on the sky impervious
to season undressing
in the wind bare
naked in the storm
faith filled communion
a commandment
as above
so below

if i want
i might fly thru the milky way
just cuz i can might take
a trip to the sun
let sun ra
baptize me in
cosmic slop &
blinding light so
supa nova style
i bleed poems
in hieroglyphics

something is always dying

something
is
always
dying
just not
in the middle of the room

they were roses before
they were mulch

five pennies in a drawer
a beggars feast is
better than an empty basket
all stories start with the potential
of happy endings
i have walked for miles
in the eye of the storm
blinded by the sun
i sought
for seven miles
i was a full moon
five pennies in my pocket

life is a dream
that ends upon waking
roses & illusions die
centuries underwater sleeping
phantoms the bones & me

sometimes death saves you
for life
roses floating on the water
five pennies in a drawer

that's the smell of hope
she said but never quite understood
metaphors dress the truth for dinner
a meal of ghost
walking on the water
mostly bone but some
have eyez
floating across the graveyard
north star eyez dream
of locomotion

transplanted trees grow
in the direction of home

my mlk walk resurrected itself on
a milk carton in
harlem
became black berets leather
coats & guns locomotion
became movement
they were roses before
they were mulch

something
is always
dying

minutes murder hours every
sunrise light cuts dark
rage & bullets next to
the hope in the drawer

bones on the water
bleeding lions onto streets
in the flow of lost religions
dangerously feeding the lumpen

baraka said every man
should see himself when
thinking of god

spotlights & sunsets
buried my five pennies
in the back of my mind next
to the chatty dead people

i wanted to be a river but
the ocean branded me one hand
a spear the other a shield
neither tool favored

the dead won't shut up
they got them pennies they
rattle them like dice
something
is
always
dying

just not in
the middle of the room

the wind won't leave me alone
got me watching fig trees
& praying to grape vines
crows & doves watch over me
knowing i too want roots
that dream drowns a
thousand times a day
sharks & itinerant poets
prophets riding dirty
godz trombones
joshua rode into
jericho with the confidence
of hannibal

i got an eight &
gin for ogun
i favor brown liquor
drums & godz of thunder
i talk to the dead
we got pennies for eyez
they rattle like dice
as we float cross the graveyard
rootless ruthlessly defying the
storm
riding on the wind
rage & bullets
in an open drawer

#we begin

spell#- 13 will become
your lucky number

i learned to fly
at mama's house
learned to
remember how
escapes are part
of my legacy a dead
lady told me my eyez
would grow later but
i need to know how
to see now you dig
i did she said you
already know & i knew
she & some other
dead folk took an early
interest in me & sent me dreams
sleep work on things
i would put to sleep
at dawn trying to
survive daylight
to root work at night
wrapped in protection
dreams
that demanded

you pay attention
you got to move in
real time willing
things to survive to
uncover instructions
tucked deep inside
metaphors clearly cryptic
like bones
thrown requiring action
nocturnal odus
altars want construction
lucidity demanded
vigilance even
in sleep
a classroom where
metaphysicals teach
sliding in & out the
in between slip out
leave your body behind
no one can follow into
rooms with no walls
the universe is an eyeball
that's you down there
you think from above
before more up there
opens cross over into
the nowhere that leads
everywhere there is more
room inside than one

imagines whole oceans
places no light
reaches creatures never
discovered find space in
space which is endless no
end to out there
no out there
we are all
no in there
we are alone
all else is the
dream acted upon
waking like religion
you believe but i learned
to fly at mama's house
i know better

origin before black

what brings us here
starts in the middle of
the story red cloth
transitions from before
but not the beginning
when we fell through
the sky into an ancient
ocean as it is above
it is below existence
bookmarked by ocean
& cosmos without limit
stardust & tears
the ark streaked across
oceans of planets
garden of eden seeded
the begining of
a new story in
the middle of another story
nothing knows the
space before the
story of the first
story where we dreamed
ourselves before
setting sail
the first
time

fugitive

(for binta)

fugitive
sunbeam
a nickel & a nail
unaware
promise
& blessings
require dues
acceptance
want payment
in overstanding
are not yours
until claimed
remembered
after opening the
clouds & reading
open to understanding
the inexplicable
the unlikely
un captured magic
free range ju ju
wild mojo
waiting to be grasped
resting on the side
of life exposing itself
whispering
expansion
beginnings
& ending the

things absorbed by
rude landings in
places by other
shores beyond
noise dressed like
it knows directions
static foriegn impulses
come apart like sores
open to completing
sentences that
never even under
much less over stood
how i could fly know
before & predict
before passing through
they only give you
a handful of words
too many are
bound to free you
quantum leaps
into hard exits
bruising contemplations
dreams of flight
manifest means
open doors
become a key
they let some
slip by
upon leaving
smash locks throw
ropes answer when
the graveyard calls

life does come with
instructions
remember
this path leads to
the ocean
the ocean leads
everywhere
diaspora
surviving no where
everywhere
stopping at crossroads
to pray with hands
that imagine
freedom from
the story written
on cotton
waiting for the
wind to blow
listening
for drums

About the Author

Ayodele Nzinga is the inaugural poet laureate of Oakland, California. She's an arts and culture theoretician/practitioner working at the intersections of cultural production, community development, and community wellbeing to foster transformation in marginalized communities. Nzinga holds a Masters in Fine Arts in Writing and Consciousness and Doctorate of Philosophy in Transformative Education and Change. A renaissance woman, Ayodele is a producing director, playwright, poet, dramaturg, actress, performance consultant, arts educator, community advocate, and a culture bearing anchor.

Also Available from Not a Pipe Publishing

Brief Black Candles
by
Lydia K. Valentine

"In *Brief Black Candles*, Lydia Valentine attends, with passionate velocity, to questions of survivability, remembrance and the creative art of living a fully human life, even in contexts and conditions that work against that what-it-could-be. ...reading becomes a mode of witness. ... Haptic, revolutionary and unflinching, this is a powerful debut collection by a poet who does not, and cannot, 'in this time-/ in this place-', look away."
   -Bhanu Kapil

"This debut collection, written in the most truthful key available to language, uses poetic form and precise repetition to give shape, then echo, to questions of family, loss, justice and survival, seated in the frame of an America that is a long way from post-racial—the America of today."
   -Sanam Sheriff
Wherever Fine Books Are Sold

Also Available from Not a Pipe Publishing

Strongly Worded Women

The Best of the Year
of Publishing Women
An Anthology
Edited by
Sydney Culpepper

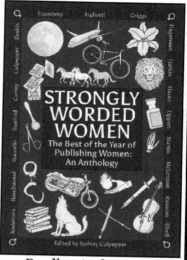

With stories by Maren Bradley Anderson,
Debby Dodds, Jean Harkin, Laura Hazan, Lori
Ubell, Chloe Hagerman, Lizzy Carney, Tonya
Lippert, Claudine Griggs, Taylor Buccello, Julia
Figliotti, Rosie Bueford, Elizabeth Beechwood,
LeeAnn Elwood McLennan, Heather S. Ransom,
Sydney Culpepper, and Karen Eisenbrey

Back in 2015, Not a Pipe Publishing announced
accepting author Kamila Shamsie's challenge to the
publishing industry to only publish women authors in
2018. After publishing eight novels by seven authors,
they capped off their Year of Publishing Women with
an anthology of 18 short stories by these amazing
women authors from across the country.
Wherever Fine Books Are Sold

Also Available from Not a Pipe Publishing

Shout

An Anthology of Resistance Poetry and Short Fiction

Edited by Benjamin Gorman and Zack Dye

With poems and short stories by **Rosanne Parry, Janet Burroway, Carolyn Adams, Benjamin Gorman, Lydia K. Valentine, Zack Dye, Rebecca Smolen, Eric Witchey, Heather S. Ransom, Joanna Michal Hoyt, Stephen Scott Whitaker, Karen Eisenbrey, Meagan Johanson, TJ Berg, Jennifer Lee Rossman, Carlton Herzog, Austin Case, Allan T. Price, K.A. Miltimore, Jill Hohnstein, Kurt Newton, Taliyah St. James, John Miller, Christopher Mark Rose,** and **Bethany Lee.**

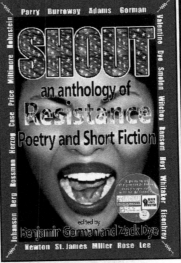

The 25 incredibly talented authors and poets in this anthology aren't politicians, policy wonks, or partisans. They're artists staring at the rising tide of fascism in the United States and asking you:
"What kind of world do you want to live in tomorrow?"
and "Who do you want to be today?"
And they aren't asking quietly.

Wherever Fine Books Are Sold

Also Available from Not a Pipe Publishing

Djinn
by
Sang Kromah

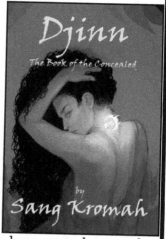

Bijou Fitzroy is strange.

As an empath, she has spent her entire life as a recluse, homeschooled by her overprotective grandmother, never allowed to stay in one place long enough to settle down and make friends. When Bijou and her grandmother move to Sykesville and she starts to attend the local high school, Bijou's world begins to crumble, town locals begin to disappear, creatures from her nightmares come to life, and she finds herself at the center of a secret war fought all around her.

"Sang Kromah weaves a tale rich in drama and TV melodrama! This is *Buffy* on acid, with all the colorful characters one would expect and more. Twists and turns - and twin heartthrobs - had me hooked from the start. A saga for the ages, and the teenagers."
  - Micayla Lally
    author of *A Work Of Art*

Wherever Fine Books Are Sold

ALSO AVAILABLE FROM NOT A PIPE PUBLISHING

When She

Leaves Me

a story told in poems
by

Benjamin Gorman

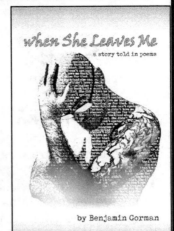

In his debut collection, Gorman relays the story of a shocking dissolution of two decades of marriage and his long crawl back to hope. Unflinching, unflattering, shocked and angry and selfish and ultimately generous, the poetry is aimed at readers open to empathy who can nourish their souls on a journey of healing.

"*When They Leave Me* is a field of wildflowers that blooms after raging fires scorch the forest. These poems not only refuse to let sorrow and destruction have the final word, they are in fact only possible because they are born from that charred past life."
-Armin Tolentino, author of *We Meant to Bring It Home Alive*

"Gorman's voice bravely explores the pain that comes with the realization that ending what was meant to be a lifelong relationship at times is the best happily-ever-after one can hope for. I honestly couldn't put this work down."
-William V.S. Tubman III, author of *Anthem Mantra Light: Poetry/Inspiration*

Wherever Fine Books Are Sold

ALSO AVAILABLE FROM NOT A PIPE PUBLISHING

21ST CENTURY COASTAL AMERICAN VERSES

BY

ZACK DYE

Zack Dye's powerful debut collection travels from sea to sea, shining a light on the ways our country's systems of oppression twist our sense of identity, freedom, love, and loss into an American mythos we wear like a hairshirt. Dye's unique experience as a white-presenting Mexican American, as a person who has climbed up and down the socio-economic ladder, and as someone who has lived and traveled across the country, produces a unique voice, sometimes pulling the reader in, sometimes shoving us away angrily, leaving us shaken.

"Zack Dye's poems channel Walt Whitman, if the American everyman had been writing more often from a place of blazing rage. With verses that can encompass both the immensity of time and the wonder of a jelly donut, Dye's collection speaks to our struggle to stay human in a pixelated world."
-Eliza Stricland, Senior Editor at *IEEE Spectrum*

"The song of a self with calloused feet and open heart, tumbling and vulnerable, raw and hopeful, inescapably honest."
- Brandon Keim, author of *The Eye of the Sandpiper*

Wherever Fine Books Are Sold